Animal Colors

Maria Koran

AV2 WORLD LANGUAGES

Published by Lightbox Learning Inc.
276 5th Avenue, Suite 704 #917
New York, NY 10001
Website: www.openlightbox.com

Library of Congress Control Number: 2023933398

ISBN 978-1-7911-5565-0 (hardcover)
ISBN 978-1-7911-5566-7 (multi-user eBook)

Printed in Guangzhou, China
1 2 3 4 5 6 7 8 9 0 27 26 25 24 23

042023
102322

Project Coordinator: John Willis
Designer: Mandy Christiansen and Sushant Deshpande

Every reasonable effort has been made to trace ownership and to obtain permission to reprint copyright material. The publisher would be pleased to have any errors or omissions brought to its attention so that they may be corrected in subsequent printings.

The publisher acknowledges Alamy, iStock, and Minden Pictures as the primary image suppliers for this title..

Animal Colors

In this book, you will learn about

- what they are
- what they are for
- which animals have them

and much more!

Animals can be many different colors. A rhinoceros has thick gray skin.

Some animals get their color from their fur. A mountain gorilla has black fur.

An orangutan has orange fur. Its fur covers almost all of its body.

One kind of animal can have different colors. Black bears can have black, gray, or brown fur.

Some birds have very colorful feathers. Peacock feathers are shiny blue and green.

A flamingo has pink feathers. The color comes from the small animals it eats.

Colors can help an animal stay safe. An iguana is green. This color helps it hide in plants.

A ladybug is red and black. Its bright color lets other animals know it tastes bad.

A lion has yellow fur.
This helps it hide when
it hunts in tall grass.

ANIMAL COLORS FACTS

Many **baby ducks** are **yellow**. They **change color** after about **six weeks**.

A **zebra** has **black** and **white** stripes. No zebras have the **same stripes**.

A **cuttlefish** can **change its** color to **hide** from other animals. This takes **less than a second**.

Tigers are orange with black stripes. They are the **only cats** with striped fur and skin.

There are **35** kinds of **toucans**. Different toucans come in **many different colors.**

A **polar bear** actually has **clear fur**. It looks **white** when **light hits it.**

KEY WORDS

Research has shown that as much as 65 percent of all written material published in English is made up of 300 words. These 300 words cannot be taught using pictures or learned by sounding them out. They must be recognized by sight. This book contains 37 common sight words to help young readers improve their reading fluency and comprehension. This book also teaches young readers several important content words, such as proper nouns. These words are paired with pictures to aid in learning and improve understanding.

Page	Sight Words First Appearance
4	a, animals, be, can, has, different, many
7	from, get, some, their
8	all, almost, an, its, of
11	have, kind, one, or
12	and, are, very
15	comes, eats, it, small, the
17	help, in, plants, this
18	know, is, lets, other
21	when

Page	Content Words First Appearance
4	colors, rhinoceros, skin
7	fur, mountain gorilla
8	body, orangutan
11	black bears
12	birds, feathers, peacock
15	flamingo
17	iguana
18	ladybug
21	grass, lion